STA
SONIC

THE ULTIMATE GUIDE TO THE WORLD OF
SONIC THE HEDGEHOG™

Chris Beckerson
25/12/93

FANTAIL BOOKS

Published by the Penguin Group
Penguin Books Ltd, 27 Wrights Lane, London W8 5TZ, England
Penguin Books USA Inc., 375 Hudson Street, New York, New York 10014, USA
Penguin Books Australia Ltd, Ringwood, Victoria, Australia
Penguin Books Canada Ltd, 10 Alcorn Avenue, Toronto, Ontario, Canada M4V 3B2
Penguin Books (NZ) Ltd, 182-190 Wairau Road, Auckland 10, New Zealand

Penguin Books Ltd, Registered Offices: Harmondsworth, Middlesex, England

First published 1993

1 3 5 7 9 10 8 6 4 2

Made and printed in Great Britain by
William Clowes Limited, Beccles and London

Acknowledgements
Photographs: p.3 space illustration of galaxy (The Telegraph Colour Library); p.5
laboratory (Tony Stone); p.29 scrambled eggs (Anthony Blake);
p.72 hotel (Topham)

STAY SONIC

THE OFFICIAL SEGA™ HANDBOOK

MIKE PATTENDEN

FANTAIL

CONTENTS

INTRODUCTION

Hey!

Don't believe we've met. (You were probably moving too slowly). You know my name, Sonic – Sonic the Hedgehog, and I thought I'd set the record straight on a few things before we go any further. So hang around for a millisec.

When the folks at Sega asked me what I thought about doing a book, I said, "You expect me to hang up my red sneakers and take up writing? No way!" They said, "But all these peo-

ple out there want to know where you come from, what you do when you're not out collecting rings, or running 'em round Robotnik, they want to know the thoughts of 'Chairman Sonic' and the inside line on your Sonic powers." So I told them OK – I'll do it – but you get it written – I'll just introduce it. So here goes:–

First, I am not a hero – I'm a Superhero. And I'm not like those other vid guys. They may claim to be super, but how can they be with that face fur moustache stuff? No, I am the original. I didn't even want to be great, I just am. What else could I do? Once Robotnik went robo-berserko – I had to save my friends – lucky for them I saved the planet too.

Now about my speed. Sega reckon they sweated bits to bust my moves through the sound barrier. Yeah, that's true, but who pushed the outside of the envelope at the last nanosec – yours truly! How? Just check out the power sneakers for maxxed-out speed. Now they all wear 'em down at Sega.

And what about the hair. It's blue, it's natural, it's cool. Why spikes? Simple aerodynamics. When you're movin' at top speeds you don't want anything to hold you back. Also – ever try a Super Sonic Spin without spikes?

OK – so that's enough from me – because you've got a whole book about me, and I've got work to do. You relax for a millisec and...

See ya in the Green Hill Zone.

IN THE BEGINNING THERE WAS SONIC

Well it happened like this,
DocKintoborwasgonnaridtheworldofevilandoneminutehe-
wasfinethenextminutetherewasanexplosionandhewastryingt
okillSonicandtheemeraldswereeverywhere.

Was that too quick? Sorry, playing *Sonic – The Hedgehog* does that to you. Hang on while we take a deep breath and hit the button.

Somewhere, tucked away on the outer fringes of the universe there's a small planet. It's barely big enough to see from a couple of million miles, let alone the 117.63222

x

light years it is from Earth. It's so far away in fact, that if you were to focus on our choking sphere from there, you'd see rock dinosaurs roaming around. It's a colourful and friendly looking orb that once gave off most excellent vibes—but we'll come to that soon.

If you go looking for Mobius (assuming you can find the right dimension and hire a 4x4 Photon Stratocruiser) you won't find it without the precise directions, which are not available.

However, if you did manage to find it, you'd be pleasantly surprised to discover a world largely unspoilt by heavy industry, urban planning disasters, skiing jackets and Jason Donovan records. One of the hippest spots – according to the brochures – is the Green Hill Zone, a sort of cross between a West Indies island, the Maldives and Kent. It's a kind of paradise, a heaven on Mobius – a smart place to chill out. Or it used to be, until Doctor Ovi Kintobor lost his mind.

Mobius was sparsely populated – one of its more attractive features – but among its inhabitants was a brilliant scientist totally dedicated to his work of ridding the planet of evil. Like any other place Mobius had its good and its bad so Kintobor, a philanthropic genius, had spent 15 years devising a machine that would contain all the evil that existed and neutralize it. But just as he was about to achieve his dream, everything went very, very wrong. One minute everything was cool, the next Mobius had become a very unhealthy and 'eggy' place to be. And it happened like this...

Scene 1

Whhooooooosh. Clunk.

Sonic untucked his head, tumbled forward a few more times, then bounced stylishly to his feet, topping it off with a mild flourish just in case someone was watching.

'Where am I!!!?' he wondered, blinking his eyes in the harsh glare of a bank of overhead strip lights, that illuminated what seemed to be some kind of underground room.

A few moments previously he had taken a short cut through a hillside near his hideaway, something he often did to save time.

'Something tells me I'm not in the Green Hill Zone any more!' he muttered to himself, staring at the immense, white-tiled room. But before he had time to shake–check the shape of his quills, a voice boomed out from behind him.

'Well, well, look who's dropped in! Erinaceus Europaeus!'

A trim, moustachioed man in a white coat loomed over Sonic and peered at him closely as if examining him. Sonic had been called many things in his life, not all of them repeatable, but he hadn't a clue what this bizarre character was going on about.

'Are you alright?' he asked. Before Sonic could answer the lab coat had walked over to a giant bank of terminals that looked like the control console of a satellite substation and begun tapping keys frantically. 'I have just one more setting to enter...'

'My name's not Aceeus – it's Sonic!' announced our hero, not quite sure whether he had been insulted. 'Where are we? What's all this gear?' he demanded, pointing to the bank of buttons, dials and lights that were flashing on and off like a Vegasian fruit machine about to pay out a lifetime's credits.

'This!' the man said triumphantly, as he patted one of the terminals fondly. 'This is the controller for my Cogwinder Retractable Particulant Corer – a CRPC to you. I'm using it to search for emeralds. Found six. Looking for the seventh. Then my work'll be done!' He seemed to have a lot on his mind and few words to waste. He punched one more key and glanced at another enormous control panel at the far end of the room, where a further bank of red and

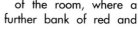

green lights danced and
ribbons of paper spewed
from a printer.

Sonic eyed the man suspi-
ciously. It was obvious the dude was
some sort of genius, or totally wacko — probably both.
Sonic zapped across the gleaming floor of the lab, taking
in the dazzling array of contraptions lined up along the
walls, on top of counters, and piled high on the shelves. He
touched one small device gingerly, it was labelled in
scratchy biro 'Cryonic Oscilloscope'. Moving further down
the line, more bizarre inventions were piled against each
other. One labelled 'Proboscile Defoliator' looked suspi-
ciously like mechanized tweezers. Sonic grimaced and
walked on surveying the reams of papers marked 'Patents
Pending' which were stacked high and the heavy leather-
bound books with titles like *An Idiot's Guide To Quantum
Physics* which were scattered around. He picked up a clip-
board covered in indecipherable algebraic notes and
doodles of improbable devices. A bold, red-ringed note
inscribed 'MONDAY: SHOPPING' stood out prominently.

'What's happening with all this stuff? Who are you!?'
Sonic demanded, tapping his foot with impatience. He was
used to being paid a bit more attention than this.

'Curiosity! How I love curiosity! You have the makings
of a top-notch scientist if only you can hold on to this
admirable quality!' the man declared, now giving Sonic his
full attention.

'My name, see here,' he pointed to the tag on the lapel
of his stiffly starched lab coat, 'is Dr Ovi Kintobor, but you
can call me Dr K. We're in my secret lab, which, between
you and me, doesn't exist!' he winked conspiratorially. 'My
mission is to rid our planet of evil and for now, that's about
all I can tell you. Unless, of course, you can help me find
The Grey Emerald!'

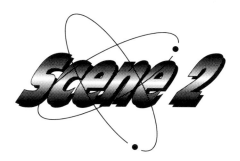

Following their accidental meeting Sonic began paying frequent visits to Kintobor's underground hideaway. The lab was a fascinating place, and Sonic loved hanging out there – watching experiments, taking in bits of information, and even picking up a few of Dr K's theories on physics. The Doc also explained his plan to rid Mobius of evil in more detail which he described as "precipitous but imperative", leaving Sonic none the wiser.

It began it seems with the greatest technological breakthrough since anti-static fluff removers and games consoles: the Retro-Orbital Chaos Compressor™ (ROCC), which – by a process too complicated to outline here without reference books, diagrams and a large supply of chocolate, crisps and fizzy drink – attracted and transferred evil from one object to another. Put simply the ROCC consisted of thousands of gold rings that constantly flowed good karma around the machine's core as it moved evil from one object into another.

Through empirical research (well trial and error actually) the Doc had also discovered the perfect objects for the transfer – six emeralds, which he named the Chaos Emeralds™. Being one bright dude he always copyrighted his inventions immediately – after all you've got to live haven't you?

At considerable risk to himself Kintobor succeeded in

transferring most of the world's evil into the emeralds, but the process had rendered them highly unstable. They would blow at any moment without some form of control. It was a problem which greatly troubled him until he came across the existence of a seventh Grey Emerald. This, when linked in parallel to the other six, could neutralize their violent forces. The trick was to find the Grey Emerald, because although he could prove its existence, he hadn't been quite able to pinpoint its exact whereabouts (in fact he didn't have a clue). Which is where Sonic was to prove so useful – or so the Doc hoped.

To aid his search Kintobor installed PCs throughout the zones of Mobius so that anyone passing by could input information that might lead to discovery of the Grey Emerald. He even offered a small reward by way of a five night break for two in the Green Hill Zone as an incentive. He also spent all his waking hours (which were considerable, he believed sleeping was a waste of valuable time) making the ROCC ready to transfer the last bit of the world's evil into the Grey Emerald and stabilize the Chaos Emeralds.

Partly out of curiosity, and partly to assist Dr K in his research, Sonic put in several hours a day on a solar-powered treadmill that the Doc had built for him. The treadmill, or Kinetic Gyratosphere™ to give it its patented name, was capable of revolving at high speeds. Sonic protested that it made him feel like a gerbil on steroids. However, when Kintobor developed special friction-reducing trainers for him he became more interested. The cutting edge design and classic red styling hid some state-of-the-art additions including Duratex™ soles with exceptional grip and specially cushioned odourless inners. Covering as much ground at the speeds he did frequently left him with blistered feet. They were also a necessary safety measure because Sonic started to build up the sort of static that could ignite the treadmill or shoot sparks into the lab. Gradually Sonic increased his speed to 200, 400, then 500 mph.

Kintobor torqued up the treadmill every day, pushing it in 20-mile-an-hour increments. What had begun as an idle exercise was developing into a majorly phenomenal experiment. Then one day, impossibly, Sonic crossed all known limits of mammalian acceleration and broke the sound barrier. The treadmill had been running for thirty-five minutes and he was little more than a blur when suddenly there was an enormous bang and a tremendous wind swept all the papers into the air. Alarmed, Kintobor attempted to slow down the treadmill – stopping it dead would have had disastrous consequences, probably sending Sonic into orbit over Mobius. Eventually he managed to gain control of the machine and gradually reduce Sonic's velocity, but it took nearly an hour to bring it to a stop.

When, finally, Sonic stepped breathlessly out of the treadmill he wasn't the same hedgehog that had gone in. His physical appearance had changed dramatically. Instead of his unexceptional, greyish-brown shade, most of

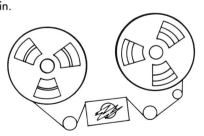

Sonic's body had turned brilliant, cobalt blue, and his spikes stood straight back in a stiff mohawk.

'My word!' exclaimed Kintobor, struggling to comprehend what had just happened. 'I think you've gone blue from the shock waves. Not to mention the Cobalt Effect!' he said.

'You clocked up 761 miles per hour! You've really earned your name now! In fact, I should call you SuperSonic – what do you think of that!' Kintobor cried, dancing around the lab like a demented, er, scientist.

'SuperSonic, yeah – radical. Cool,' grinned Sonic, examining his glowing blue body proudly in a mirror, 'but what about getting some food? All that running's made me hungry!'

And with that, the subject of the most revolutionary kinetic experiment in history went out for a double cheese burger and large fries.

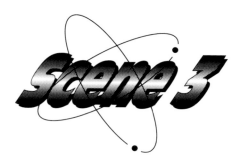

Scene 3

A couple of months passed with Sonic's appearance showing no sign of reverting back to its former drabness. Nor did his speed decrease as he surged all over the place covering large distances in the hope of locating the Grey Emerald for the Doc. He hadn't been round to the lab in fact for a week, what with the overwhelming attention he'd been receiving from his friends since his transformation, so he decided to drop in one afternoon.

Doc Kintobor had been continuing with his experiments without let up. In fact he had been so engrossed in his research that he hadn't even noticed Sonic's absence. While he was pleased to see him he immediately returned to his work leaving Sonic to read his favourite comic *Attack Of The Killer Zombie Penguins*. Some time later (Sonic wasn't sure quite how long – he only ever carries a digital stopwatch) Kintobor came over.

'I feel a bit peckish, I think I'll knock up a quick snack. I don't suppose you'd say no either?' Sonic, never one to turn down food, opted for a triple-decker cheese, salami, salad, pickle, mayonnaise and mustard sandwich. The Doc trailed over to the fridge he kept in the lab. It was empty. In fact it almost always was, he rarely remembered to eat which was why he was so thin. 'Oh, dear!' he declared, 'I haven't had time to get any food in recently. We can share this though,' he suggested proffering a hard-boiled egg from the otherwise empty cabinet. Sonic walked over and took the egg.

'Porgghhh! This totally stinks, Doc – it must be ultra rotten!' he said handing Kintobor back the egg and gripping his snout tightly.

'It can't be, it's only been in there six months,' said Kintobor examining it as he wandered over to the ROCC and began tapping in yet more commands. But Kintobor wasn't concentrating – not very sensible when you fiddle around with an ROCC – and he miskeyed some numbers without realising. Suddenly there was enormous spark and the lab was engulfed in a cloud of smoke.

After what seemed like an age the smoke cleared to reveal the Doc sprawled on the floor. Sonic stood coughing in the middle of the acrid mist. He peered through it at a rotund figure who bore no resemblance to his friend. Doc Kintobor had been totally changed by some awful, freak accident. The once slim scientist had been transformed into an obese blimp and there was a peculiar eggy niff hanging in the air. In fact it smelt like the toilets of one of Earth's busier curry houses.

The most bizarre aspect of the metamorphosis was not only Kintobor's ghastly, egg-like appearance, but the letters on his name tag which had been mysteriously reversed.

'Dr Ivo Robotnik,' Sonic mouthed, reading them in

stunned amazement. The Doc looked up, a dark scowl spreading across his bloated face.

'What are you gawking at, you ugly blue porcupine! Stand still so I can rip out your spikes and turn you into an armadillo-bot!' he growled.

'Whoa! What's got into you?' Sonic yelled, jumping back.

'Don't you understand, you little spiked rat? Get back to your rodent hole! It's over. You're finished! I'm in control now and I shall rule Mobius forever!'

Clearly the Doc wasn't feeling himself, and there was something in his manner that suggested to Sonic that he'd better tread carefully, play along with him a bit.

'Oh yeah? And how're you gonna do that?' he probed.

'The Emeralds – it's all in the Emeralds! Now I am evil like them. Beautiful, symmetrical and unstoppable. I shall launch them into space and they shall help me control the world. And no one, no one will ever find the Grey Emerald. NO ONE!" Robotnik was frothing at the mouth with delusions of grandeur. Then he realized he'd put his mouth into gear before engaging his considerable brain.

'Now you know my plan you little walking pincushion! YOU SHALL BE EGGS-TERMINATED!!' and he suddenly lunged at Sonic.

But Sonic was too fast. He bolted out the back door of the lab and headed for the Green Hill

Zone to warn his friends, his ex-mate's curses echoing behind him.

So — just to bring you up-to-date — the formerly good, if somewhat daft, Kintobor had become the hopelessly evil and utterly egg-centric Robotnik, a megalomaniac with an unstoppable mega desire to control Mobius.

There's probably some tedious moral in the whole sorry story but there's no point in crying over spilt rings. So what exactly happened to throw Mobius into total confusion? If we rewind to the point where the Doc was hamfistedly tapping at the ROCC keyboard with the egg in his hand we can run it by in slow motion and grasp the full impact that a couple of transposed digits can have.

So there he is a slim, nay svelte scientist tapping at some keys when suddenly there is a giant blue spark and:

a)   The ROCC goes into meltdown and zaps the Chaos Emeralds, Kintobor, and the rotten egg in his hand.

b)   The ROCC begins to transfer some of the evil stored in the Chaos Emeralds to Kintobor, changing him into the evil Dr Ivo Robotnik.

c)   Robotnik immediately takes on the physical characteristics of the egg, expanding to grotesque proportions.

d)   The ROCC explodes, scattering its golden rings throughout Mobius's zones. Phew!

If that's not a big enough mess to deal with, Robotnik, as he must now be referred to, decides that megalomania is this lunar year's thing.

And Robotnik is no dummy. He quickly realizes that to succeed in his plan, he must destroy the only creature who knows his scientific secrets — Sonic. Suddenly it's open season on hedgehogs.

Cursing the extra speed he helped his former friend build up, Robotnik devises a multitude of traps which he places throughout Mobius's zones. He also captures many of Sonic's friends using them as bait, or transforming them into robots programmed them to attack him. It's a grisly business which Robotnik thoroughly enjoys.

As for the Chaos Emeralds, Robotnik turns them into satellites and launches them into orbit over Mobius. Circling high above the planet, the emeralds enhance Robotnik's power over Mobius. As an added precaution, he launches a psychedelic Warp of Confusion (Secret Zone) around each emerald. Only the Grey Emerald can neutralize the forces of the Chaos Emeralds and render them harmless.

Despite his entire world falling apart within the space of a few hours Sonic didn't contemplate slashing his paws. He isn't the type to let his head drop. With everyone turning against him he went into hiding, but quickly came to the conclusion that Robotnik must be destroyed if his friends were to be freed and Mobius restored to its former state.

On the way, he resolved to recover the Chaos Emeralds from the Warps of Confusion. Robotnik did his worst, transforming several areas of Mobius into no-go zones – beginning with Green Hill and continuing through several parts of the planet once considered worth hanging out in.

But no matter how devious the traps Robotnik cooked up Sonic was equal to the test, risking life and limb to free his incarcerated pals and pursue the fat freak to the final confrontation. His victory (recorded in *Sonic 1*) seemed to signal an end to the nightmare that had begun in Kintobor's laboratory, but of course Sonic had only won the first battle – the war had a long way to run.

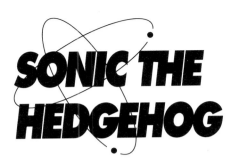

SONIC THE HEDGEHOG

Some are born great as they say, others have greatness thrust upon them. Sonic falls into the latter category – forced to become a hero when Robotnik snatches his friends and threatens to put Mobius bottom of everybody's holiday itinerary.

SONIC YOUTH

No-one is quite sure how Sonic arrived in the Green Hill Zone. He was found wandering around in a daze one day by Sophocles, a sharp-eyed owl. A number of different possibilities have been suggested, though there is little hard evidence to support any of them. Quite simply, one day he wasn't there, the next he was.

*   *   *

Whatever the reason Sonic refuses to speak of the incident now, claiming he was too young to remember. What is known is that Sonic grew up in the forest, surrounded by many animals who befriended him, passing on many of their inherited skills. Sonic rapidly picked up different tricks and characteristics from them, which were to come in much more useful than he ever imagined.

Johnny Lightfoot, a rabbit and Mobius's undisputed sprint champion at the time, coached Sonic, and soon he was able to outstrip every other creature in the forest.

Sally Acorn (the squirrel) taught Sonic how to leap incredible distances – a skill that has proved vitally important in combat with Robotnik.

Mobius is covered with a great deal of water. Sonic became equally adept in aquatic conditions after he met Joe Sushi (the unfortunately named walrus) while paddling along the shore one day. Sushi demonstrated how to dive and swim underwater. Tux, a lone penguin who was separated from his fellow pals when an iceberg broke away from the mainland and carried him to the

Green Hill Zone, taught Sonic how to control his breathing underwater for long periods.

But it was purely by chance that Sonic developed one of his most useful attributes: the Super Sonic Spin Attack. It happened when Chirps, his terminally cheery young chicken pal, began learning to fly. He stood on the edge of his nest claiming that he would fly on his first attempt and promptly tumbled head over heels onto his beak. Sonic fell over too – laughing.

When Sonic did the same thing he built up so much velocity he became a revolving blur of spikes. Next thing he'd drilled a hole through the side of a mountain! With practice Sonic found he could do it with ease and accuracy. In fact it became a useful source of taking short-cuts.

This is how he first encountered Dr Kintobor, boring by mistake into his lab one day. Despite finding the Doc somewhat mystifying, Sonic took to him immediately. Sonic's inquisitive nature meant he learnt a great deal by hanging out with his highly-educated friend and he was happy to take part in the many experiments Kintobor devised.

SONIC STYLE

Sonic is instantly recognisable with his striking blue spikes and his trademark red trainers. (That's, of course, if you catch him standing still on a rare moment.) Usually all you see is a radical blue and red blur disappearing into the distance.

Sonic's only physical failing is his trouble coming to a stop once he's running at supersonic speeds. Despite his low slung centre of gravity he occasionally moves too fast to maintain good balance, and has to struggle to keep from falling when he comes to the edge of a cliff.

FOREST SMART

Sonic thinks he's perfect, but he's not. Forest-smart, Sonic is of average intelligence, making his IQ about half that of Kintobor's. He has to struggle to figure out the solution to a problem or puzzle. Ask him the cube root of 356634 and you might have to wait a couple of months for an answer, but question him on speed-climbing techniques and you'll find a world authority.

Usually, he relies on his great charm and tremendous physical ability to get him out of tight spots. Sonic never analyses a situation, he just plunges in. He's a hedgehog of action, a doer not a thinker.

PURE CHARACTER

Stubbornness and cockiness are just two of Sonic's traits, along with 'forest smarts' (comparable to 'street smarts') a sixth sense where danger is concerned and an innate understanding of life in the open. Carefree and radically cool – that's what Sonic is all about.

Patience is not one of his strong points, nor is being ignored. He is a natural showman, never happier than when he has an audience for his stunts and practical jokes. Sonic thrives on attention.

Then there's the Sonic Attitude. When he wants something, he goes for it – 150%. Sonic does not respond well to authority. He's cocky, outspoken, independent and self-assured. Generally it's his mouth that gets him into trouble. One more thing about Sonic's personality – he's more than a bit vain. His spikes are always perfectly straight.

In Sonic's world, slobs finish last. His red trainers are always spotless. They don't get much of a chance to pick up dirt, but when they do look marked, Sonic cleans them up. They're so designed, thanks to Kintobor, that they don't smell either. Sonic is particularly sensitive to bad odours – one of the reasons he always knows when Robotnik is in the vicinity.

TASTY

Sonic's diet is high in cholesterol to fuel his tremendous speed. He loves burgers, tacos, nachos, fries, anything chocolate, and cola by the gallon. It doesn't sound particularly healthy, but Sonic is constantly on the move and burns

up calories at an amazing rate. Diet drinks and high bran, lo-fibre foods are not his style.

Sonic loves speed and enjoys any way of experiencing it, but when he does slow down, there's nothing he likes more than racking up a top score on his Game Gear. His superb paw-to-eye coordination makes him a crack games player. You won't catch him playing puzzle games though, he can't stand them. He also has a large comic collection, favouring superhero mags.

The need for speed is never absent for long with Sonic and he can be very tetchy when held up. If the action slows down he's liable to make ironic gestures, yawning, or tapping his toe in exasperation. Sonic likes nothing more than exploring new places. In fact he's pretty damn nosy which, he accepts, gets him into some sticky situations.

WORLD VIEW

Sonic's objectives in life are to have fun and enjoy the ride! Not too complicated a philosophy really. Life is a blast, if you don't stop to think about it and that just about sums up Sonic's worldview. As long as he has his supersonic speed, his sneakers, and his friends, Sonic is one happy dude – two out of three though is not good enough. Friendship is crucial to Sonic, he's never happier than when he's hanging out with pals (as long as he's the centre of attention). Take that away and he's your worst enemy.

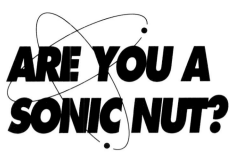

ARE YOU A SONIC NUT?

TO BE THIS GOOD TAKES AGES, AS THEY SAY, SO JUST HOW COMMITTED ARE YOU? COMPLETE THE FOLLOWING QUIZ AND FIND OUT...

1) Your best friend is playing Sonic II on your Megadrive when you notice he is about to top your coveted high score. Do you:
a) Sneak quietly downstairs and throw the power switch and claim you have just been cut off for not paying the bill?
b) Applaud loudly, clap him on the back for being a stout fellow and give him your signed Guns N' Roses 12-inch as a reward?
c) Throw him out and refuse to speak to him ever again?

2) You overhear a group of people making negative remarks about Sonic II. Do you:
a) Agree with them, sell your system the very next day and take up collecting matchboxes?
b) Point out politely that they are leading sad, empty lives and show them why with a display of technical games wizzadry?
c) Drop your kecks on the spot and proffer them both cheeks?

3) You are having a quiet night and a game of Sonic when your girlfriend/boyfriend rings up to announce she is coming round and wants to watch Ghost/Terminator II for the seventh time. Do you:
a) Cut the video cable, put the machine in a cupboard and

claim you have been burgled when he/she arrives?

b) Accuse her of going out with the Chippendales/him of going out with the Dagenham Girl Pipers and finish with her/him forthwith?

c) Order pizzas, settle back and wait for the pottery scene/special effects?

4) It is your dad's birthday. On the way to buy him a present, you notice that Sonic III has just hit the shops. You only have enough money for the one item. Do you:

a) Snap up Sonic III, punch yourself in the eye, roll in some mud and claim you were mugged?

b) Buy him a Black & Decker power drill and get a video games magazine with the change?

c) Stop off at the bookies en route and slap your hard-earned on Mr Snodgrass in the 3.30 at Chepstow?

5) Your mum accidentally pulls the plug out of your Megadrive as you are about to rack up a truly momentous score. Do you:

a) Shed a small tear, but console yourself that you'll clock up another biggie next go?

b) Tell her she's a dozy old trout and go and upstairs to pack your bags?

c) Fiddle the high score table and add a bit extra on for your troubles?

SCORES

If you answered a) to any question award yourself a chubby three points for each answer.

If you answered b) have a couple for good measure.

Choosing c) gets you a paltry un point.

12-15 points: You are Sonic bonkers, an unsaveable games nut – but do you have any social life?

8-11 points: You are a loyal Sonic fan and will receive your due reward when they dish out the high scores in heaven

5-7 Did you buy this book at a car boot sale or something?

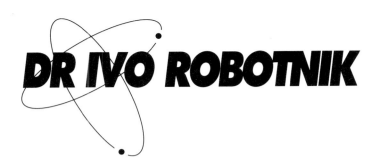

DR IVO ROBOTNIK

Before his unfortunate accident Dr Ivo Robotnik wasn't an evil scientist with an egg-shaped physique. No, he was Dr Ovi Kintobor, a kind, gentle and slim man of science with a finely-honed mind who spent 15 years conducting experiments to improve life on Mobius. What went wrong?

EARLY YEARS

Kintobor's CV makes for impressive reading. Little is known about his family except that they were unremarkable in every sense and that he was adopted. The names of his surrogate parents aren't recorded, probably since his achievements rapidly overshadowed them.

At eighteen months, young Ovi was able to perform complex algebraic calculations and beat mainframe computers at 3-D chess. By the age of four he was holding lengthy discussions on subjects ranging from molecular structure to team selection and tactics for the World Speedball Championships. He also picked up five different languages – including Phoebian, Semmelweisian and Ursan – by dialling interplanetary videochat lines and clocking up a hefty bill in the process. He developed a habit of reciting lengthy passages of Dzonghan poetry leading his parents to believe he was mad. Instead, after extensive tests, he was judged to have an IQ of 268. Child psychologists suggested plenty of external stimuli and cutting back on the E1666 in his diet.

Apart from a minor incident which involved the scrambling of a neighbouring planet's starfighters after he hacked into their defence system, Kintobor enjoyed a trouble-free childhood. One excerpt from his school report suggested Kintobor "has outstanding ability" though it added "must try harder". Aged nine Kintobor patented his first invention, a molecular egg stain remover – the first sign of what was to become a major obsession later in life.

Robotnik went on to obtain every advanced scientific qualification possible from all eleven universities on Mobius.

At sixteen he enrolled at the University of Syraceuse where he published a report questioning accepted theories of thermodynamic entropy. His tutor was subsequently dismissed and Kintobor instated as head of department, where, with a sizeable grant, he began research into advanced cybernetics. He left Syraceuse to set up his own research and development business from which he invented over a hundred devices – such as osmatic spectacles – now accepted as everyday eyewear all over the universe and electronically adjustable platform shoes.

When his business collapsed during the great Syraceusian slump Kintobor returned to Mobius declaring philanthropically that he intended to devote the rest of his life to the defeat of evil. He disappeared from sight refusing all interviews and was rumoured to be working on a major project – in fact nothing was heard from him for 15 years.

News of a terrible accident at his underground laboratory was confirmed by his transformation into Doctor Ivo Robotnik, an obese and utterly unpleasant egg-ocentric bent on the destruction of Mobius and Sonic.

PHYSICAL CHARACTERISTICS

Once a trim man given to a healthy organic diet, Robotnik is now disgustingly rotund, with a decidedly egg-shaped physique, a grotesquely evil face and worst of all, a moustache. In fact, he's bad and mad, with spindly arms and legs stuck onto an egg-shaped torso. He is bespectacled, bald, and bulging out of his labcoat. Plus, he has a major league body odour problem, which makes him smell like a rotten egg – but that's nothing compared to the noxious odours which emanate from elsewhere. It is not a good idea to point this out to him.

His happy round face conceals a seriously unbalanced mind and often results in people seriously underestimating him. This is compounded by his oily egg-regious manner which suggests he is about to do you a big favour when you first meet him. In fact, he is about to brainwash you and turn you into a mechanical zombie. His pyschotic personality is nevertheless quite comical – just don't let him catch you laughing.

Naturally Robotnik is more than a little slow on his feet – in fact he can't even see them. Running is out of the question, but then he has the Egg-omatic.

MENTAL ABILITIES

In line with his physical resemblance to an egg, Robotnik is definitely cracked. Unfortunately, he still possesses nearly all of his formidable intellect, which he now puts to work for evil purposes. He further augmented his mental capacities by embedding a ceramic neural network in his brain to carry out physics calculations in his sleep.

Robotnik's transformation into a devious genius follows in a grand tradition of inventors gone wrong. Earth had Dr Frankenstein who constructed a being called Tony Adams from stolen parts of dead bodies and Dr Jekkyl who utterly transformed his personality with super strength lager. The planet Ursa was home to Professor Krank, who spent thirty years trying to measure the speed of light with a stopwatch and a tape measure.

PERSONALITY, WHAT PERSONALITY?

Robotnik is nasty and stark raving mad – in fact the word 'sociopath' may have been invented for him. He does not hesitate to destroy or control any creature who stands in the way of his plan to take over Mobius.

He has also developed an obsession with becoming the most infamous psychopath in history, although he has some way to go before he achieves his aim. For example supermarket king Rudi Bonkerz annihilated the entire population of Betelgeuse, by declaring they were a delicacy and shipping them to processing factories to be pickled and exported. A mentally disturbed war hero General Krutch from Nkruma wiped out an entire solar system when he detonated a star with a bazooka and several supernova shells.

BAD TASTES

Robotnik has always adored, and still adores eggs – hard-boiled, scrambled, over easy, poached, or in an omelette. Now, he especially enjoys them raw, with a dash of tobasco. He eats with his hands, chewing with his mouth open so that he frequently loses bits, leaving yellow eggy stains on his white lab coat. His personal hygiene leaves a great deal to be desired. He doesn't wash and never cleans his teeth so hideously are they stained. His breath smells... of egg.

To unwind, Robotnik likes to watch endless horror movies in 3-D. He cheers and applauds loudly at the goriest bits. He enjoys reading obituaries and horror stories.

Robotnik dislikes just about everything, particularly the countryside, animals, trees and fresh air. He hates Sonic. Also, Robotnik realises that Sonic knows many of his scientific secrets and is onto his plot to control Mobius. This has left Robotnik permanently with egg on his face.

Yummy! Robotnik's favourite breakfast

OBJECTIVES IN LIFE

After the accident, Robotnik came to the sudden realisation that understanding Nature wasn't enough - he had to dominate, control, and contort it. And so his goal in life became to control and/or mechanize anything he came across since then. He has cultivated a hatred of the environment and dedicated his life to conquering Mobius.

THE EGG-O-MATIC

Because he is so disgustingly obese, Robotnik has trouble seeing his feet, walking any further than the front door, and standing for long periods of time. He installed elevators in the lab so he didn't have to climb its many stairs, widened the door frames and reinforced the toilet.

His answer to his lack of mobility is not to go on a crash diet but to build a spaceship, the Egg-O-Matic, which he molded perfectly to his bulbous body, and in which he can zip around the zones and launch attacks on Sonic.

The Egg-O-Matic is fast, it has to be if he is ever to catch up with the supersonic one, and it is armed with a vast array of weapons to be deployed on Sonic when he does catch up with him.

After delicate negotiation with Robotnik we can bring you an exclusive artist's impression of the Egg-o-matic's cockpit.

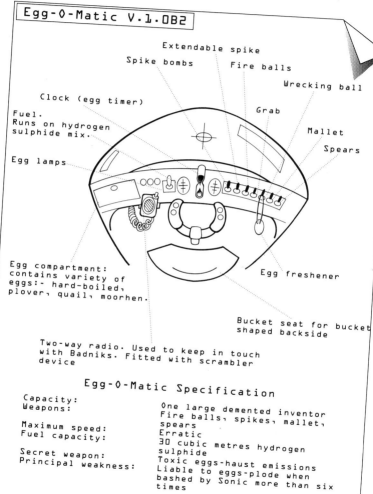

Egg-O-Matic V.1.0B2

Extendable spike

Spike bombs

Fire balls

Wrecking ball

Clock (egg timer)

Grab

Fuel.
Runs on hydrogen
sulphide mix.

Mallet

Spears

Egg lamps

Egg compartment:
contains variety of
eggs:- hard-boiled,
plover, quail, moorhen.

Egg freshener

Bucket seat for bucket
shaped backside

Two-way radio. Used to keep in touch
with Badniks. Fitted with scrambler
device

Egg-O-Matic Specification

Capacity:	
Weapons:	One large demented inventor
	Fire balls, spikes, mallet, spears
Maximum speed:	Erratic
Fuel capacity:	30 cubic metres hydrogen sulphide
Secret weapon:	Toxic eggs-haust emissions
Principal weakness:	Liable to eggs-plode when bashed by Sonic more than six times

ROBOTNIK'S BADNIKS

Robotnik's deviant mind has balked at nothing – not even merchandizing and reprogramming virtually every animal found on Mobius to attack Sonic and Tails. The animals are still trapped inside the robot suits, and Sonic has to smash them gently to let his friends out safely. This is the low-down on the bad guys whose sole mission in life is to nick Sonic.

CHOPPER

This fiendish fish lurks under bridges in the Green Hill Zone, leaping straight up out of the water to attack anyone who passes. Robotnik has fitted it with razor-sharp teeth, armoured fins and a nasty temper.

MOTO BUG

A motorised insect with a particularly nasty overbite, it hangs out in the Green Hill Zone giving the green fly nightmares. Repellents won't stop the Moto Bug, but its steady speed and lack of armour mean that it's an easy target for Sonic.

CRABMEAT

A selfish shellfish with claws like bolt croppers. It's a slow mover, but every so often it stops to change direction – or to fire ball-bombs into the air. Crabmeat often hangs around with a pal, and can be found in the Green Hill Zone and Spring Yard Zone.

BUZZ BOMBER

Another of Robotnik's robot insects, and the first one to attack from the skies. Buzz Bomber is easily beaten but possesses a fatal sting which fires diagonally downwards for quite a distance. Sting it before it stings Sonic! Buzz Bombers plague the Green Hill Zone, Marble Zone and Spring Yard Zone.

NEWTRON

Fierce lizard-like creatures, Newtrons come in two breeds: the Lesser-Spotted Blue Newtron, and the Lesser-Spotted-Oh-Heck-It's-That-One Green Newtron. They're both lesser spotted because they hide on walls, perfectly camouflaged. When someone passes, Blue Newtrons fire a ball-bomb and disappear again, waiting for another victim. They can be found – with difficulty – in the Green Hill Zone.

CATERKILLER

Based on the idea of a harmless caterpillar, Robotnik created this lethal slow-moving pest, forever inching towards its prey. Only its head can be damaged as each spine carries a fatal poison. Don't let Sonic attack it while it's turning round and be careful when it explodes. In fact, don't attack it if Sonic can jump over it.

BATBRAIN

Batbrain hangs around on roofs in the Marble Zone. Any movement wakes it, and it will flap down noisily to investigate. Beating one or two of them is easy for Sonic, but he's wary of larger flocks – especially if there's a Caterkiller around as well.

ROLLER

A bizarre-looking creature, based originally on a flightless bird but now mechanized almost beyond recognition. Robotnik's Roller is never good news. Sonic jumps over it while they're rolling, and attacks it as it stops and opens up – but he's very careful as this roller can flatten him. Thankfully it's only found in the Spring Yard Zone.

SPIKES

Less of a hermit crab and more of a harm-it crab, Spikes is a weird blend of Moto Bug and Crabmeat and lurks on rooftops in the Spring Yard Zone. Although its pink shell is easily recognised, its spiky rear and fearsome fore-claws make it one of the Zone's least desirable pets – unless you're a mad scientist, of course. It enjoys hanging its fore-claws over the edges of buildings for any unwary animals who may be jumping upwards. It can only be damaged by a hit to the head.

BURROBOT

Happy underwater and on dry land, Burrobot lives in burrows in the Labyrinth Zone with only its spinning drill nose showing above the ground – until it leaps out and attacks. Its caterpillar treads can climb steps and make it a fearsome opponent. The best way to annoy it is to call it a sissy and knock off its baseball cap.

JAWS

Just when Sonic thought it was safe to go back in the water, Robotnik perfected Jaws – a fish with a chip on its shoulder and a mouthful of teeth that will bite through six inches of solid hedgehog. It doesn't have a favourite colour (it doesn't have a favourite anything) and its hobbies include swimming and biting anything that moves. It lives in the watery depths of the Labyrinth Zone.

ORBINAUT

Orbinauts are extraordinary creatures. Part animal, part machine, all nasty, they can be found underwater in the Labyrinth Zone, on dry land in the Star Light Zone and in the Hilltop Zone in *Sonic II*. They come in all colours, some of them throw four spiky missiles, some have missiles but don't throw them, and some don't even have missiles (Sonic's careful of those ones because they can't be killed) but they all have a middle bit with big eyes, and they are all slow-moving. If Sonic sees an Orbinaut, back away from it. Jump over the missiles, then attack. If they don't throw their missiles, Sonic jumps over them.

BOMB BOTS

Robotnik's most fiendish creations, Bomb Bots are the only Badniks without an animal inside them – they have a kilo of explosive instead! They look friendly and dozy, but if Sonic gets too close, the antennae on their head will start flashing and then Sonic gets three seconds before they blow up.

Sonic hates packs of them because they set off a chain-reaction. They're found in the Star Light Zone and the Scrap Brain Zone.

BALL HOG

With its snout-like nose, the Ball Hog is primed to sniff out hedgehog, and it can be a real swine. It lurks at the end of corridors in the Scrap Brain Zone, spitting bouncing bombs at anyone who comes close. Sonic's never rash here, and saves his bacon by attacking it as fast as possible.

SONIC II BADNIKS

When Sonic saw off all Robotnik's Badniks in *Sonic I*, the demented inventor had to come up with another crazed crop to help him conquer Mobius again. Here are the names of the latest lot of murderous machines to take on Sonic – and lose.

BUZZER

A close relation of the Buzz Bomber, in fact it's an updated model, Robotnik ironed out the faults of the first one making this one faster, more accurate and a much deadlier pest than before. It flies around the Emerald Hill Zone, loosing off missiles and making life hell for picnickers.

MASHER

More fishy business from Robotnik. Masher is a large freshwater relative of Jaws, that

only feeds on ... hedgehog! As there's only one hedgehog in the Emerald Hill Zone, where Masher lives, it's desperate for a decent meal and leaps out of every pool and waterfall, trying to snatch a mouthful with its nickel gnashers.

COCONUTS

Designed to make a monkey out of Sonic, this cheerless chimp shins up and down the palm trees of the Emerald Hill Zone, lobbing fruits and nuts at passers-by. Offering it a cup of tea only makes it angrier, so Sonic waits until it's just thrown something and then takes it for a spin – a spin attack!

GRABBER

An aggravated arachnid that will grab anything that passes in its steel legs. Sonic squashes the little blighter before it can squeeze all the rings out of him and wrap him in its nylon web. Some people have wondered why there aren't more Badniks in the Chemical Plant Zone – it's because Grabber isn't very discriminating about who it grabs.

SPINY

A bizarre little limpet-creature which slides slowly along, occasionally opening its top to half-heartedly lob out a missile. It clings tenaciously to the floors and sometimes the walls of the Chemical Plant Zone – about the only Badnik that Grabber can't pick up and bundle away.

WHISP

Like a microlite version of the Buzzer, the Whisp is a household pest gone very, very wrong and needs swatting double-quick. Whisps hang around in gangs in the Aquatic Ruin Zone, teasing the dozy Grounders and beating up innocent bluebottles. Sonic spins like crazy when they're around and they get the message.

GROUNDER

The grumpy elder brothers of the Burrobots from the Labyrinth Zone, Grounders hide in walls and hillsides in the Aquatic Ruin Zone, jumping out when Sonic least expects it.

CHOP CHOP

One of the nastiest aquatic inhabitants dreamed up by Robotnik, this fast, mean and brutal barracuda from the Aquatic Ruin Zone goes wild at the scent of hedgehog. Sonic's very careful, lest he gets canned by the tuna. If you thought it was impossible for something to have big teeth and a brain – think again.

CRAWL

Encased in a titanium shell, only Crawl's head emerges from its armour, and it's quick to protect that with its shield when it's attacked. Its claw snips and snaps at anyone foolish enough to attack from the front, so Sonic's forced to do the unsporting thing and spin into it from behind.

REXON

One of Mobius's oldest inhabitants, Rexon is a dopey dinosaur with a prehensile neck, which has only survived this long by being lava-proof, spitting ball-bombs at its enemies, and living in the healthy and stress-free environment of the Hill Top Zone. Its head is vulnerable to attack, and its body can make a useful stepping stone.

SPIKER

Spiker looks like the middle of an Orbiton on four crab-like legs and wearing a dunce's cap. It scuttles along floors and ceilings in the Hill Top Zone, shooting its spiky headgear at anyone who jumps over or runs under it. Once it's done that, it's defenceless.

FLASHER

If you're a sightseer in the picturesque Mystic Cave Zone, don't miss the bright lights of the Flashers, switching on and off like beacons. If Sonic is trying to get through it, he avoids them like – well, like Flashers! They're nasty when they're off, but he tries not to get close when they're turned on and hot for action.

CRAWLTON

Crawlton is the biggest creepy-crawly on Mobius. It loves the dank atmosphere of the Mystic Cave Zone and lurks in bushes and behind walls, shooting out its long neck at anyone who stands still around it. Luckily its reactions are a little slow, but Sonic doesn't wait around – and never steps on it in case it bites his feet off.

OCTUS

Half octopus and half helicopter, this oily creature only uses its eight tentacles for hovering in mid-air while it fires a ball-

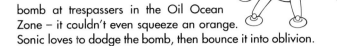

bomb at trespassers in the Oil Ocean
Zone – it couldn't even squeeze an orange.
Sonic loves to dodge the bomb, then bounce it into oblivion.

AQUIS

This spiny sea-horse from the Oil Ocean is no thorough-
bred. It flies fluttering its fins, and fire bullets frighteningly
fast… Sonic sometimes dashes underneath it (it's a steep
old chase) and attacks from there.

ASTERON

There's only one real star in *Sonic II* and this isn't it.
Asterons sit on walls in the Metropolis Zone waiting for
someone to come past – and when they do, the star-shaped
creatures explode, loosing off five missiles in different directions. Sonic and Tails can't destroy Asterons, they can only
avoid their shots. Luckily these shooting stars have to wait so
long between visitors that many of them are fast asleep.
Only the ones that move are dangerous.

SLICER

The martial mantis of the Metropolis Zone, Slicer hurls its
boomerang fore-claws at approaching enemies. If it misses,
the claws fly back and it tries again – but it is defenceless
while the claws are in the air. Sonic can dodge them,
squash the bug and they'll fall harmlessly to the floor.

SHELLCRAKER

Crabmeat's bully of a big
brother, Shellcraker waits for
victims in the maze of the

Metropolis Zone. Its spiky front claw shoots out on a long chain, but Sonic can avoid it by remembering this simple advice: Shellcraker can't turn round.

TURTLOIDS

They look slow and old as they fly through the Sky Chase Zone, but Sonic doesn't mock these mutant turtles or he'll end up in the soup. He likes to knock out the little pilot and use its low-flying ancestor as a platform.

NEBULA

Not one of Robotnik's better ideas, Nebula is full of hot air and the propeller on its head is just for show. Sonic doesn't like to get underneath it, in case he sees stars. The Sky Chase Zone would be better defended by a squadron of Buzz-Bombers than by this hopeless lot.

BALKIRY

This big bird has a laughable Concorde-like nose, and is fast, furious and fairly feeble. Sonic doesn't recomend trying to ride on this Balkiry.

CLUCKER

Apart from Robotnik. Clucker is the only inhabitant of the Wing Fortress Zone, where it pops up in its machine-gun nest. It has the same problem as Shellcracker – it can't turn round. Once on its blind-side, and Sonic can choose whether to scramble its egg or pull its wishbone at his leisure.

SONIC II MEGADRIVE TIPS

**AN INDISPENSABLE GUIDE TO TACKLING ROBOTNIK'S
LATEST THREAT...**

In all this format of Sonic II has eight main stages
(Emerald/Chemical/Aquatic/Casino/Hill Top/Mystic/Oil
Ocean/Metropolis). Seven of these have two sub-stages
while the eighth stage has three sub-stages. These coupled
with the special stages, where you get a chance to collect a
Chaos Emerald, give a grand total of 24 stages if the game
is played straight through.

EMERALD HILL ZONE/BOSS 1

Not too many problems here until your first encounter with
Dr Robotnik. Position yourself at the far left of the screen

and wait for him to come on-screen and link up with his spiked car. Then when he comes at you jump up and land on him. If you don't bounce off him too high you can get in two hits as he goes by you. Then run right and he will chase you from the right, again wait for him to get quite close to you and jump up and land on him being careful not to bounce off him too high so you can get two hits before he passes you.

Repeat the procedure twice more and his car will go up in a puff of smoke and he'll fly off. Jump on the pad to free your friends and complete the stage.

CHEMICAL PLANT ZONE/BOSS 2

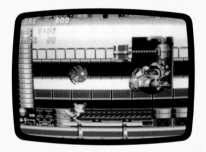

You can pick up an extra life if you drop into the highly corrosive Mega Mack at the bottom right of the screen just before you face Robotnik. Move sharply you don't have long down there.

Position yourself close to the far left making sure the flipping tiles won't swallow you and wait for him to appear from the right. He will now attack you by filling up the water container above his ship and dropping it on you. To destroy him wait for the water container to move directly over your head. Push the pad to the right and leap to ram his ship, the water bomb will miss you and his ship will flash, then go to the far right of the solid strip and wait for the water container to fill up again. As he manoeuvres it over your head again dodge left and ram his ship and wait at the far left. Repeat this seven times and his ship will explode and fly away. Be careful as you leap over the flipping yellow panels on the right. Land on the solid section and jump on the metal case to release all the animals.

AQUATIC RUIN ZONE/BOSS 3

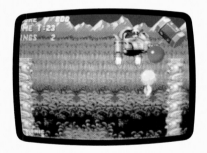

Once you reach the end of the final stage two totem poles will rise up on each side of the screen. Stand in the middle of the screen and Robotnik will drop down above you with a big mallet attached to his ship.

To beat him you have to avoid the arrows fired from either side of you, and ram his ship. Because his ship is so high above you, wait for the arrows that fire from each side to lodge in a totem pole and then run and jump on them to ram his ship. After you've rammed him seven times his ship will blow up and fly off. Go right and release your animal mates from the pad.

CASINO NIGHT ZONE/BOSS 4

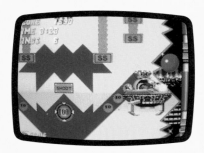

Once you have flipped through the end of the final stages go to the far left corner and wait for Robotnik to position himself above your head. When he's stopped quickly run to far right and position yourself slightly up the curved wall. Press down any button and keep holding it down until he's shifted to the upper left of you. Before he stops above you release the spin attack and you'll climb the side wall. As you go up push gently to the left so you land on his head or upper part of his ship. You will come zooming down the steep wall quickly so move over to the left side and again position yourself slightly up the steep wall and push down on any button so you are ready to do a spin attack when Robotnik appears to the upper right of you. Again, after you have hit him, quickly regain control and run to the far right side and repeat the above steps by preparing a spin attack and releasing it when he appears to the upper diagonal of your position. Hit him seven times to defeat him.*At all costs don't trigger the flippers as you move around or you can die very quickly!

HILL TOP ZONE/BOSS 5

Go to the far right corner and position yourself at the far left edge of the platform you're on. Robotnik's ship will rise out of the lava below you. Drop down and bounce attack him. Use small bounces and don't press the button too long, so that you can get in three or more attacks in one go.

As he starts to go back into the lava make sure you bounce off him and land on the ledge to the left and drop down to the next ledge. His ship will lob a fire bomb onto the ledge to your right, wait for it to go out and go back up to the ledge to the right. Wait for Robotnik to surface to your left and fire a bomb at you. Jump over it. Robotnik will lob another fire bomb onto the ledge to your right but stay where you are because he'll appear to your right again. Bounce off him as many times as possible and he'll go back down and appear to your left. Jump over the bullet he fires and wait for him to appear to your right again.

After hitting him seven times he'll explode and you can run right and release the animals from the steel cage.

* If you should lose all your rings and, subsequently, a life you'll restart at the star post. Don't go right, instead go left and collect four rings and then go to the far right to face Robotnik again.

MYSTIC CAVE ZONE/BOSS 6

This boss is relatively easy to destroy. All you have to do is position yourself about four inches from the far right wall and just look up. Rocks and jagged spikes fall from the ceiling. The rocks will pass through you and do no harm but unfortunately the same can't be said for the spikes.

Just sit tight and look at the top of the screen. If a spike appears directly over you gently touch the pad left or right. When Robotnik appears make sure you have some distance between yourself and him and wait for him to drop his spears and come at you, then jump up and land on his head.

Go to the opposite side of the screen and wait for him to disappear and another set of rocks and spikes to drop, then as he moves towards you bounce on his head again. If you time it well, you can get two bounces in on each attack. Go to the other side of the screen and wait for him to disappear. Let the next set of rocks and spikes finish and repeat the attack moves. The trick is not to panic, and watch directly above you and gently touch the control pad to slip away from any falling danger.

When Robotnik is beaten go right and break the steel cage and free your friends.

OIL OCEAN ZONE/BOSS 7

Go to the furthest platform on the right and then walk to the left of the platform you're standing on. Wait for Robotnik to appear below you in the oil. When he does bounce down onto him. Be careful not to bounce too high off him by holding the button down too long as you hit him. The shorter the press the quicker you can drop back down on him and the more hits you can make.

Go to the far right of the screen. A hooked arm will come out at you. Wait until it is near you and jump straight up and over the head of it, its body cannot harm you. A snake-like gun will come out of the oil and jiggle around, watch it closely and if its laser is pointing at you then leap straight up. When it has fired and disappeared back into the gunk move to the edge and wait for Robotnik to appear and bounce on him again. Repeat the process again, waiting for the hooked arm to come out.

If you want to take out Robotnik very quickly, jump down into the oil and keep pressing a button so you bounce on the surface when Robotnik is about to appear. You can ram him in the oil about five times before he drops beneath. When he drops away bounce back up onto the platform to the right.

After you hit him seven times he blows up and you can go right and break the steel cage and release your friends.

METROPOLIS ZONE/BOSS 8

It's quite easy to beat Robotnik if you follow a few simple rules here. He enters from above so go to the far left corner and wait there. When he comes at you wait until the circling balls around his ship are almost up to you then make the highest possible jump over them and run to the far right side of the screen and wait there. When Robotnik moves over to you, jump over him and go to the far left side and wait there.

Robotnik will go to the centre of the screen and the balls will expand around him. When they shrink back to his ship and are moving horizontally around him, run across and ram the bottom of his ship. He'll go up and release one of the balls which will fall to the ground and bounce around. Spin attack this and then go to the far left corner and wait for him to come down again. Repeat the previous moves until he's lost all his rotating balls. He'll then go up and down the screen firing lasers from his ship. Avoid them and ram his ship once more to explode it.

Go right and break the steel cage to release all your animal friends.

WING FORTRESS ZONE/BOSS 9

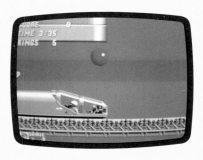

Go past the star post and continue right until you find a small cone shape in the floor in front of you, jump on this and it'll break to reveal a gap in the floor. Drop down through it and go right. You'll drop down some steps.

Collect some rings as you go. You'll see two red beacons, one above your head, the other directly below it on the floor. Jump over them and collect the rings between them.

You'll then be confined between two yellow beams, one to the right the other to the left. To defeat Robotnik you have to wait for three spiky platforms to drop down from the ceiling and begin to move around the screen. Follow their path carefully and jump onto and between them and ram the red part which comes out of the grey metal dome on the ceiling. Watch out though as the grey metal dome will glow and fire a vertical beam that can kill you. If you touch the spikes on the moving platforms you will be killed too.

This is one of the toughest bosses in the game. You must be patient and take your time as you have to ram the red part of the dome eight times to destroy it. A general tip is to try and stay on the ground until the vertical death beam from the dome has stopped, then jump up onto a spiky platform and try to ram the dome at least twice before it fires its beam again.

Also quickly recover any rings you lose if you are hit as you are going to need them to beat this tough brute of a boss!

When you beat the dome go right over the red beacons and drop down and go right and you'll see Robotnik fly off in his ship to the right and you'll stop at the far right end of the ledge. Tails will then appear in a plane and you will automatically leap on top of its wings.

The action then scrolls up vertically where Robotnik's ship is hovering. You'll automatically jump off and grab onto the engine of his ship. When you are holding onto part of his engine on his ship the vertical scroll will slow down and you will find the ship docks and you're into the Death Egg Zone for the final confrontation.

DEATH EGG ZONE/ ROBOTNIK HIMSELF

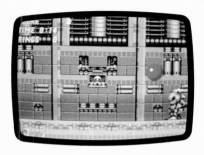

When you appear in this stage go right and you'll drop down into a closed-off chamber. Go to within three inches of the far right corner and wait. An evil looking Sonic made of stone will float down from the ceiling on jet boots. When he lands quickly get in a couple of hits by jumping on him, then move back off to the left. Be very careful because if you land on his spinning spiky head you'll lose a life!

Go to within three inches of the far left and wait for him to curl up into a ball and spin very quickly to the left. Jump straight up and he'll stop to your left, in the far left corner. Wait for him to change into stone and jump on him.

A good tip here is to watch the speed his blades are rotating and when they're just about to stop jump a frac- tion early so you have two chances of ramming him. Quickly leg it to the far right of the screen and he'll run straight at you at ground level. As he gets near leap back to the left over him and he'll stop at the far right. Quickly jump back at him and you should get two hits in, if you're tight on your control. He'll then run back at ground level to the far left and you can leap over him and ram him twice more. He then curls into a spiky ball and leaps in an arc above you to the far right of the room, so stay near the centre right and when he changes from a spiky ball to a stone Sonic again ram him twice very quickly. Repeat the process until he explodes.

You can then run right and a door will close behind you, another door in front of you will open up and you can see Robotnik in front of you, running to the right down a corridor. Follow him down it and you will see that he runs and jumps into a dome. Don't touch it or you'll die.

Move back to the left and wait for Robotnik to rise up out of the floor in his huge Robotnik suit and walk towards you. To destroy him you have to ram his stomach sixteen times. Be ready when he goes off the top of the screen – you'll see a sight appear on the screen trying to zero in on you. This is where Robotnik will land back down from the top of the screen so make sure you're nowhere near this spot. When he lands he releases some small Robotniks that will run out at ground level and try to ram you. Ram them to take them out. Also keep well away from Robotnik to avoid his extending arm sections that fly quickly at you.

You have to be very patient here. Remember you must hit his stomach 16 times and this can only be done when his spiky arms are clearly to his side, avoid him at all other times and take out the nasties he drops. Destroy Robotnik and you are treated to a stunning end sequence.

SONIC II MASTER SYSTEM TIPS

AN INDISPENSABLE GUIDE TO NEGOTIATING THE HAZARDS OF SONIC II

There are seven stages in Sonic II MS (Underground/ Sky High/ Aqua Lake/ Green Hill/ Gimmick Mountain/ Scrambled Egg and Crystal Egg). The six Chaos emeralds are carefully hidden. They appear in sub-level two of each main stage and if you fail to pick up all five then you'll get a shortened ending on Stage Six. If you have found all five then destroying the Mekka Sonic on Level Six will allow you access to the final level and the chance to rescue Tails.

While the main stages are quite easy to get through the bosses are a different proposition. You only get one chance to take them out. There are no rings to collect, so one mistake means instant doom.

Here are the tactics and moves needed to beat the bosses and Robotnik in the final encounter.

UNDERGROUND ZONE/BOSS 1

Leap over the mine cart, run down the steep hill and take a flying leap to the far right and you'll land on a ledge with a lava pit to your left. Run at the wall to your right and push down when you are close to it, and you'll break through, continue right and up until you see a spring in the wall to your right. Jump up and land on it. At the top run quickly to the right, down a steep hill and take a flying leap at the bottom. Robotnik will swoop down saving you from the lava pit and will place you on a ledge high above.

He will release you on a small hill to a beastly brute with nipping claws at the bottom. The claws have to be hit six times by the bouncing ball that appears from the right. Stand exactly where he dropped you and when the ball approaches simply jump up as high as you can and it will pass under you landing on the claws.

Jump over six balls this way and Robotnik will appear. Jump over him as you did with the balls and he'll go to the far right and take out the claws, now you can run right. Go to the far right, and jump up and ram the Robotnik ship to release all your animal friends!

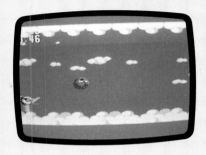

Ram the spinning turtle and keep moving right until you see the clouds. You can safely leap right onto them. Wait in the middle of the screen and you'll see four small chick robots spring up from below, two to the left and two to the right. Bounce on them to destroy them.

Another four robot chicks appear in the same way. Use the same technique to destroy them. When you have beaten the second set of chicks you fall through the cloud to another set of clouds below where four pods release more robot chicks. Take out the two pods to your left with bounces, then carefully bounce onto the two robot chicks to your right and keep going right and bounce out the other two remaining pods.

When all the pods and chicks have been beaten, a metal-lic-looking bird head will appear and start to fire at you. If you spend too long taking out the pods they keep releasing chicks and the metallic bird head will appear. If this happens concentrate on taking out the pods and chicks before going for the bird head.

The trick is to ram the bird head and not get hit. When you hit the bird head it knocks you back to the right. You must control the bounce off it with your D pad to avoid its bullets. These bullets will home in on you but you can out-manoeuvre them. Hit the head six times to beat it and ram Robotnik's ship to release all your furry friends.

AQUA LAKE ZONE/BOSS 3

Take a running jump. When you get to the other side leap over the horizontal red spring. You'll go down a steep diagonal hill. As you reach the bottom don't fall into the water, just leap across to the ledge to your upper right. Go right and drop down onto the red horizontal spring, roll into a ball and it will push you through a solid wall to your right, keep going and drop down into the water. Keep going down to the right and eventually you will see a big air bubble appear onto your left, leap up into it and push lower left diagonal to avoid the spikes overhead, then push upper right diagonal to avoid more spikes. At the top go right and drop down onto a red spring this will push you up and out of the water. Go right at the top and you come to another of Robotnik's robot bosses. Get quite close to him and wait until he starts to blow a bubble, then as he flips his head to vertical, jump and land on the bubble on his nose. Repeat this six times to beat him, then ram Robotnik's ship to release your animal friends..

GREEN HILL ZONE/BOSS 4

Go right until you get to the green vertical spring, leap onto it and push hard right on the D pad. As you start to come down you'll see a tree. Drop down next to it and you hit another green vertical spring. Repeat the process.

You land in an enclosed vertical section with spikes to your left and a green spring underneath you. Jump off this green spring onto the ledge above you and then drop down to the right to another green vertical spring. If you scroll the screen down you'll see a green vertical spring to the right and below you, ignore this. Instead take the green spring after the first drop off the ledge to the set of three green vertical springs onto your immediate right. Get across to the third spring to the right and land on the ledge next to it. Then, carefully drop down to your right to a single green spring. Jump off this to the right and you land on a long ledge. Continue right and make your way slowly down a long, steep diagonal ledge, stopping every few steps. At the bottom you see a set of three green vertical springs. Jump right onto them.

To make it to the ledge you must have forward speed, that is, when you jump off the third spring to the right at the bottom of the steep diagonal you must make the jump to and from the three springs high up to your right as one continuous jump.

If you do this you make it to another set of three green vertical springs, jump off the third one along and keep pushing hard right on the D pad and land on a ledge at the far right hand side.

Continue right and you will find the fourth Robotnik Pig Robot boss at the far right-hand side. He curls up into a ball and leaps high over you. When he lands he stands still and you can ram him and then back off. Repeat six times to destroy him. His moves are random every time so the best place to be is the ditch in the middle of the screen.

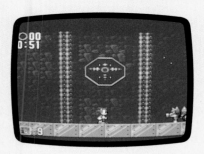

Drop down the vertical shafts until you can leap onto the conveyor belt. Run and leap off it to the right and repeat the process over four more conveyor belts and then leap up onto a platform that will take you up.

Jump off the platform onto a spring to your upper left and then land on a platform to your upper left again. This takes you up, changing direction before it gets to the spiked ceiling. Go right and up through the gap to your right. As you go up take the first left off the platform. Wait for the platform to come down, leap onto it and then leap up onto three steel blocks. Go left and drop back down onto the platform and stay on it as it moves left and down.

It will go down and left across a wide section of spikes. At the far left it falls away, so leap left onto the spring there and jump up and to the right to a ledge and prepare right for your fifth encounter with a Robotnik boss!

You see a spiky-shelled pig to your far right, position yourself so you're standing in front of the pillar to the left. The pig turns and runs at you. Jump over him. As he rams the wall to your left he releases small shells from the top of the screen that fall down. Avoid them and you'll see the spikes go back into his body. Ram him quickly and avoid the falling shells from above. Run to the right of the screen and position yourself in front of the second pillar from the right and wait. The pig will run to the right and you can jump straight over him.

When he stops, jump and ram him and then move over to the left of the screen in front of the far left pillar again and wait for him to charge. Don't try to ram him as he'll only pull his spikes in for a short time. Instead move over to the second pillar on the right again and wait, when he charges again jump over him and ram him. The distance he bounces back from the wall will vary so always give yourself a reasonable space and also make sure you do not bounce too high or off at an angle when you ram him. You can avoid the falling balls easily if you make a small bounce off the pig and move slightly to the side of it. Then run to the other side of the screen waiting for its next attack. After six hits he dies and you can release your friends from Robotnik's ship.

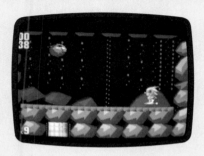

Jump on the spring at the far right and go up into the funnel above you. Don't follow the split to the right, unless you want to get spiked. Bounce off the springs onto a ledge to the right, leap over the spikes and you'll see a ledge with four vertical springs. Walk across them, leap and land on the first spring to the left and shoot upwards through a ledge. Jump on the spring on a ledge above you. Push right and you'll hit springs in the wall to your right and shoot upwards. At the top push left and land on a hanging platform. Quickly jump up into the funnel above it.

Follow the many twists and turns and you'll end up in a chamber with the Silver Sonic. To beat him, ram him when he is standing straight. If he is curled in a ball and you hit him you'll just bounce off him. Ram him eight times. A good technique is to keep jumping and while in mid-air twist and turn so that you land either on or near him so it is easy to ram him.

If you haven't collected all five Chaos Emeralds you won't be given the ending sequence here. If you have all five, Silver Sonic will give you the sixth and you can proceed to the seventh stage.

CRYSTAL EGG ZONE/
ROBOTNIK HIMSELF

Drop down a funnel, go right and you'll find yourself in a chamber with Robotnik. Jump into the funnel to the left and circle around the outside of the room while Robotnik releases bombs into the middle of the room. These will slowly home in on you. Wait until the bombs have almost expired and he releases the yellow zigzags. When they have gone through the floor stop circling the room and come out of the funnel in the floor and push hard right and up so you hit him by landing on top of his head. Then go into the funnel in the left wall and repeat the process eight times.

Watch out for the lightning flash in the room itself as this will kill you if you're in the room. Enter the funnel where Robotnik was sitting, go through another and you'll see Robotnik running right. Follow him as he goes, into a special overhead chamber. Lightning flashes will light up the screen and he will disappear. Tails will float down and start smiling as Sonic shakes his hand.

SONIC CELEBRITIES

THEY ANSWER THE QUESTIONS THAT MATTER...

CATHY DENNIS

What and where was your first ever experience of
Sonic?
*Jumping in the box which goes under the water into the
spinning aura.* (Weird)
Who would you cast to play Robotnik in a film?
The guy who played Jaws in the Bond movie Moonraker.
If you ever met Sonic what would your first question be?
Do your spikes ever need sharpening?
Where would you take Sonic for lunch?
A jewellers with a lot of rings.

RICHEY JAMES (MANIC STREET PREACHERS)

What and where was your first ever experience of Sonic?
Guildford, July 1991.
What was your worst Sonic moment?
Guildford, July 1991.
What was your funniest Sonic
moment?
None, it's a deadly serious business·
Most frustrating thing about Sonic?
Waiting for Sonic III

ZAC FOLEY (EMF)

What and where was your first ever experience of Sonic?
Rockfield Studios in Monmouth, Gwent.
What was your worst Sonic moment?
I had nightmares in which I asked Sonic to go out with me and he agreed.
What was your funniest Sonic moment?
Meeting Mrs Sonic and her children. (Nice)
Can you think of a suitable Sonic motto?
Sonic the spiky ball.

RICHARD FAIRBRASS (RIGHT SAID FRED)

What was your most bizarre Sonic moment?
When he jumped out the console and ran across the carpet.
Who would you cast to play Robotnik in a film?
James Woods.
What would be your first question if you met Sonic?
Don't you get cramped in there?
Most frustrating thing about Sonic?
He doesn't speak French.

TOM HINGLEY (INSPIRAL CARPETS)

Who would you cast to play Robotnik in a film?
Lionel Blair.
Most frustrating thing about Sonic?
Unimportant things stopping me from playing like my wife, kids etc.
Where would you take Sonic to lunch?
Corley motorway service station, there's always plenty of hedgehogs there! (Sick)

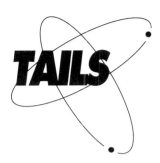

TAILS

ROBOTNIK ONCE SAID HE WOULDN'T GIVE TWO EGGS FOR SONIC'S PALS. WELL, IN FACT, SONIC'S FRIENDS AIN'T TOO KEEN ON ROBOTNIK. AND WHEN THE GOING GETS 'EGGY' FOR SONIC, TAILS IS ALWAYS THERE TO HELP HIM OUT.

EARLY TAILS

A young fox born on Mobius, Tails had always looked up to Sonic and dreamed of being like him. But he was luckier than most people in one crucial thing – he knew Sonic. It's not everyone that has a jet-propelled superhero for a pal, but then again they're thin on the ground.

Miles Prower (Tails' real name) was pretty distinctive himself, a regular everyday sort of fox from most angles, he was actually graced with two tails. One is enough for most foxes, but Miles had to go and have two. Like his hero, he was distinctive, not part of the ordinary forest crowd – maybe, he hoped, even destined for greatness, too.

Miles was instantly nicknamed Tails (people can be really obvious can't they) and took a fair bit of kidding from the other animals for his spare brush. This never bothered Tails though, he knew he was special. The others soon stopped the wind-ups too, when they saw his additional appendage enabied him to fly.

Tails discovered his ability by pure accident – literally in fact. He was climbing a huge tree in the Green Hill Zone one day, and had inched his way almost to the top, when a branch he was standing on gave way and he plummeted towards the ground. Disaster was only a second away when his tails suddenly whirred into action. He simply hovered to safety as if it was the most natural thing in the world. Further experiment proved

he could do it at will. He was *one* cool air-borne fox!

His first encounter with Sonic was memorable. Tails had learned of the daring, single-handed campaign which the hedgehog had successfully waged against Robotnik. Indirectly he felt he owed him his life. One day while hovering around on the South Island he actually ran slap into the supersonic one. Sonic, fortunately wasn't travelling too fast, so neither of them came to any harm.

'Watch where you're hovering dude!' said Sonic checking his quills were still in place.

'Sonic!' gasped Tails.

'That's my name!' said Sonic eyeing the fox inquisitively, 'Hey you've got two tails, that's cool!'

Tails blurted out his admiration for Sonic, which, naturally, Sonic enjoyed and soon the pair got to talking. A friendship had been struck up and from that point on Tails shadowed his pal everywhere, in an effort to keep up with him. Occasionally this would drive Sonic up the wall, particularly when Tails would get under his sneakers and trip them both up. Usually when the fox got too close for comfort he'd put on a burst and leave him behind. But sooner or later Tails would come helicoptering into sight with his tails spinning for all they were worth.

Sonic liked to tease his pal by zooming off or performing his Super Dash Attack, but he couldn't believe it when Tails developed a spin attack of his own. Sonic had been showing off (as usual) and Tails had been trying to imitate his pal, taking a run up and bowling head over heels. Then suddenly he picked up some speed out of nowhere and turned into a ball of red fur. He had his very own spin attack!

From then on, like it or not (and there were times when it was definitely not for Sonic) the two were inseparable. Tails and Sonic were a double act.

THAT TAILS LOOK

A red ball of fur. Where Sonic is always impeccably turned out, Tails, just doesn't have Sonic's style.

Then there's the matter of possessing two tails. This makes him doubly good at wafting away unpleasant smells and insects. Double joints at the base of his spine explain their bizarre rotary action.

WHAT A CHARACTER

Like his pal Tails is naturally inquisitive. He loves exploring, delving about and rooting around the undergrowth. He is also crafty, hanging back to see how things turn out. Blindly loyal to the point of unquestioning stupidity, Tails will follow Sonic anywhere no matter what the dangers. It's possible to conclude that Tails is more than a bit dim, but, hey, he means well and his heart is in the right place.

TASTE, BUD

Unlike most foxes, Tails' diet doesn't consist of several plundered chickens a day, it upsets Sonic, who pointed out that he might end up picking Chirps from his teeth one day. Instead he shares a diet similar to Sonic's, though he still can't resist the odd fried chicken bucket.

BREAKING THE SONIC BARRIER

In this exclusive interview, *Vole* magazine's Aseg Eporue caught up with the supersonic hedgehog who has style to spare. They talked about Sonic's life, his style and the rumours concerning a forthcoming TV show and a film based on his adventures.

Vole Magazine

In my extensive career I've interviewed the biggest stars but nothing could prepare for my first meeting with Sonic the Hedgehog. Setting up the interview took months.

This was not, as I first imagined, because Sonic prefers to remain aloof from his audience – in fact much the opposite is true, he is gregarious by nature, open and easy to talk to – but that he is genuinely impossible to track down most of the time. He never seems to be in one place long enough to accept a phone call, let alone schedule an interview. Eventually though, with some help from Sega I was able to organize a rendezvous when he stopped over on a whistle stop promotional tour.

When I finally came face to face with the supersonic star, in the penthouse suite of a five star hotel, I was amazed at his immaculate appearance. Washed and groomed, his blue spikes stiffly combed back, his eyes glinting in the light he was the very embodiment of charisma.

A hectic schedule notwithstanding, he seemed relaxed and communicative, though after only a few minutes it rapidly became clear he has a short concentration span, breaking off in mid-answer to scout inquisitively round the room or gaze out of the window as if he was looking for someone. Time was short so we got straight down to business.

AS: It's been a long wait for the second instalment of your adventures. How come Sonic II took so long?

SONIC: Well, Aseg, it's probably because I set Robotnik's plans back so much last time. In fact, we hoped he was finished, but old egg features is back and he means business.

AS: It certainly looks a tougher challenge this time.

SONIC: Yeah, I think whale belly realises he underestimated me last time, but his lame challenges don't faze me. (*Jumps across room to rummage through wardrobes and drawers*).

AS: It's something of a buddy act this time...

SONIC: You mean Tails? Well sometimes I wonder which side that dude's on, but he means well. Whatever happens though, *Sonic II* is my show. I'm still top hog.

AS: Talking of top billing, I want to ask you about the rumours of a possible film deal.
SONIC: Well, first of all there's a TV series but it could well happen, yeah! I mean if these dumb Italian waiters or whatever they do are worth a film, then I sure as hell am! Things are in planning stage at the moment, but I can tell you that I'll be playing myself – no one else could manage the stunts!

AS: This is going to make you an even bigger name than you are now!
SONIC: Could be, but that's cool. I deserve it! [*At this point Sonic leaps out of seat and peers through the window*].

AS: How do you feel about the hype and attention - people writing books about you and opening clubs named after you and so on.
SONIC: Well I'm flattered. The book sounds brilliant, though what's with the stuff on Robotnik?

AS: What is your kind of music?
SONIC: Well, basically I like anything that has a fast beat – thrash metal, rave music, hardcore. The more bpms the better!

AS: Is that what you do with your spare time?
SONIC: Well I rarely have any spare time, but when I do I play a lot of games – usually on my Game Gear. I'm pretty hot despite the fact that I don't practise much. Basically I go for anything that scrolls fast – racing sims, shoot 'em ups. The one I can't put down currently is *Road Rash 2*, it's almost as fast as I am.

AS: What about your eating habits?
SONIC: Well I don't eat in flash restaurants, the service is too slow and the food's weird, ha, ha! Generally I eat on the

move. Fast food – the faster the better and lots of it. I need plenty of calories because I burn up so much energy. My current favourite is nachos – hot and spicy and covered with loads of melted cheese. Which reminds me, I'm hungry, I think I'll send out for something. (*Leaps out of chair and grabs telephone.*)

AS: Sonic you're pretty laid back, does anything bother you?

SONIC: Well I try not to let it, but there are a few things that get my spikes up, yeah. Hanging around is the main one. Like getting stuck in queues drives me crazy. Also people who think it's clever to offer me hedgehog-flavoured crisps and make jokes like 'Why did Sonic cross the road? To see his flat mates'. If I've heard that once I've heard it a million times. Oh, yeah and people who don't respect the environment. They're a total pain.

Conversation turns to Mobius on which Sonic is notoriously unforthcoming except to say that's it's 'a cool place'. Before we can make any headway we are interrupted by a knock on the door and the appearance of a double order of burgers, extra large fries, a deep pan pizza, hot dogs and a bucket of cola which Sonic launches hungrily into. Unable to compete with this for his attention I make my way to the lift. I realise the entire interview took less than five minutes. What is it with this guy?

Vole

THE ZONE ZONE

MOBIUS HAS MANY ZONES - SOME OF THEM STILL UNDISCOVERED. HERE IS A LEVEL BY LEVEL GUIDE TO SOME OF THOSE WE KNOW ABOUT: WHAT THEY LOOK LIKE AND HOW THEY USED TO LOOK BEFORE ROBOTNIK GOT HIS EGGY HANDS ON THEM.

Once a smart, hip place to hang out, Mobius has suffered immensely at the puffy hands of Robotnik. His redevelopment plan for many of its zones (all completed without planning permission, naturally) left it disfigured and dangerously unsafe. The result was to turn one of the cosmoverse's coolest spots into a total no-go area – unless you're the sort of hardy, outdoor type who relishes the challenge of rock-hopping lava pools, examining deviant flora and fauna whilst dodging giant spikes. Robotnik let his diseased imagination run riot, and turned many zones into hell holes worse than a timeshare on a Grade One penal planet.

In *Sonic 1* Robotnik and Sonic battled it out in six of Mobius's better-known spots, beginning with what was originally their home patch, the Green Hill Zone. Robotnik's early efforts now seem half-hearted by his usual despicable standards, extending only to boring through the hillsides weakening many cliff edges so they crumbled away without warning; or installing rotating spiked tree trunks. Subsequently his work on areas like the Marble Zone, to which he imported a job lot of dungeon equipment, and the Star Light Zone, to which he brought his new-found love of pollution and industrialized blight, demonstrated that Robotnik was a force to be reckoned with.

So, too, was Sonic and his erstwhile mentor seriously underestimated the skill and determination of the supersonic hero. Consequently Robotnik never got to fulfil his warped plan and normal service was resumed. Or so everyone thought...

REVENGE IS DISCREET

After Sonic foiled Robotnik's warped masterplan to control Mobius and destroy him, the planet returned to relative normality. The zones were reconstructed and the minefield of traps and hazards was cleared. Sonic was reunited with his friends and rapidly returned to his old habits, nosing around, messing about and playing practical jokes. He even found a new friend in Tails. Everyone thought the ordeal was over, but Robotnik was still at large.

Things, however, did go quiet for a while, but it was only the calm before the storm. Everyone, Sonic included, was lulled into a false sense of security. Robotnik had merely gone to ground to plot his revenge. Working behind the scenes with his vast fortune, he began infiltrating the infrastructure of Mobius, gaining control of entire cities and factories for his own ends.

Then the disappearances began. At first there were so few that no one noticed but they spread. Soon more and more familiar faces had gone mysteriously missing. Then came the rumours, fuelled by Robotnik's propaganda apparatus – that a deadly virus was loose, animals were being sucked into space by a giant tractor beam and there had been an outbreak of spontaneous molecular combustions. The truth was far worse. Robotnik had begun work on his most devious creation yet, the Death Egg, a powerful device capable of destruction of apocalyptic proportions. He was abducting vast numbers of animals to work on its construction in an underground factory. Robot hit squads were sent out at night to snatch animals who were then drugged and transported to his factory. There neurological implants were inserted in their brains which turned them into automatons.

He had also not forgotten the damage Sonic had inflicted

on his plans last time, so he had constructed another set of zones which he placed between himself and the superfast hedgehog. Never one to admit he was wrong, he gave many of them similar themes to the zones he had constructed in *Sonic 1*. As an extra incentive to lure Sonic into his clutches he sealed many of the supersonic hedgehog's friends in prison eggs which he cleverly situated at the end of each zone. The demented prof also customised the Egg-O-Matic, adding a new set of weapons. Monitoring his progress through the zones he was now able to swoop into the attack the moment Sonic looked like rescuing his pals.

As ever, Mobius's only hope of a return to normal service lay with Sonic. It's pretty daunting to realise that the future of an entire world – and that of all your friends – lies with you (imagine being asked to save the rainforests before breakfast) but Sonic wasn't the sort to be phased by such minor considerations. And he still had the rings to provide some protection!

RING LEADER

When Robotnik's (or Kintobor's, if we're being precise with our timescale) ROCC blew its top, one of the side-effects of the eruption was to launch more gold rings into the atmosphere than an explosion in a jeweller's shop. Even a scientific slaphead like Robotnik will concede that what goes up must come down, and down they came – all over Mobius. It didn't take long for Sonic to discover that they offered some protection from the downright antisocial traps that Robotnik had devised to try and bring about his untimely end.

Back when Kintobor was still a sane, genial scientist with the noble plan of ridding Mobius of evil ("that pathetic creep of an inventor do-gooder" as Robotnik now refers to him) he had installed a network of PCs all over Mobius in the hope that like-minded citizens could enter information as to the whereabouts of the Grey Emerald.

Up to the tragic moment when the ROCC went into melt-down and Kintobor's sanity logged off permanently, it has to be said that the PCs hadn't been an extraordinary success. Perhaps it was asking too much, but all that had been entered on the hundreds of machines scattered about the place, was a stream of abusive messages, offensive poetry and a strongly-worded letter to the Mobian Daily Herald. Others thought they were bank creditpoints, local information guides or quiz machines. However after the rings came down to earth Sonic discovered that the PCs had altered their make-up, too. By an intricate molecular process far too complex to discuss here without going into immense detail, the PCs had absorbed some of the rings, while others had gained even more useful powers offering shields, power-ups for his trainers and invincibility boosts when he most needed them. They could be accessed simply by jumping up and down on them – which, you have to admit, beats using a password any day.

Nevertheless these PCs were only a minor source of comfort when Sonic began his second quest. He soon realised what he had let himself in for – a potential one-way trip through some of the most hostile environments known to man or hog. But then Sonic had to do it to get the Chaos Emeralds and to save Mobius.

EMERALD HILL ZONE

Not many people would positively enjoy turning a peace-able, laid-back beauty spot into a lethal danger zone, but then we're not dealing with a normal person here. Robotnik is a grade-A fruitcake and he is out to get Sonic.

The Emerald Hill Zone was once a tropical bay near the equator of Mobius, a tranquil haven unblemished by the sort of ugly features associated with Earth resorts like sprawling hotel developments, fun fairs and beaches packed full of tourists exposing themselves.

On the surface little had changed: the Emerald Hill Zone was too neat a place for even Robotnik to ruin. It retained much of its finest features including its lush palms, plateaus, ocean views and waterfalls. True, one or two unpleasant additions had materialised but nothing likely to trouble a hedgehog capable of travelling at the speed of sound – least of all the lame Badniks that now populated the place lobbing coconuts about. In reality Robotnik didn't excel himself by his own vile standards. Sonic didn't even have to pause for breath when he encountered its hazards – but by then reality and Robotnik were no longer on speaking terms.

CHEMICAL PLANT ZONE

The chemical plant zone is a quintessential piece of Robotnik dirty-dealing. In a secret factory he acquired, a scuzz–hole of the highest order, he began research into a deadly toxic chemical which he could employ on Sonic.

Naturally he started with the most smelly, egg-based substances he could produce. Putrid hydrogen sulphide

compounds which smelt so good to him though, that he cur-tailed this avenue of research unable to believe that anyone else would be remotely harmed by them. Instead he began to toy with more vitriolic ingredients, combining unstable substances until he struck on something utterly disgusting: megamalatricarboSonichloride – which he marketed as Mega Mack™. This glutinous pink liquid proved to be satisfyingly lethal in tests he carried out. Anything immersed in it went a grisly magenta colour and died within a minute.

One property he didn't bargain on, was its powerful corrosiveness which he discovered by chance when some barrels he filled with Mega Mack™ disintegrated within hours. Never one to waste an opportunity, he seized on the idea of flooding part of the factory with it – after all the place had served its purpose – and installing a prison egg full of Sonic's friends on a platform just over the putrid pink liquid. Naturally the tiles of the platform disappear the moment anyone steps on them. True criminal genius.

AQUATIC RUIN ZONE

In the past Mobius had been populated by some great civilizations, but there were some which had never made it off the ground, for example the original inhabitants of the Marble Zone who built a city on an unstable volcanic surface.

When this race began to lose entire cities to lava pools they gave up trying to construct there, moving on to what they assumed was a more suitable location to build on. But bad luck struck again – they had chosen an area a short distance from the coast. An unexpected shift in the landmass saw the zone drop 50 metres whereupon it was instantly submerged, drowning everyone. An underwater labyrinth of excavations was left with only carvings in some of the stones as proof that they had been there at all.

The land still changes height unexpectedly, exposing parts of the excavations without warning. Its shifting water table and unpredictable currents makes it a dangerous place, fit only for fish. The arrival of Robotnik on the scene transformed it into an undersea booby trap that pushed even Sonic to the limit. Fortunately he had taken the time to listen to the advice of Joe Sushi and Tiki the penguin which gives him an edge as he explores the vast sunken passages. But not even Sonic can hold his breath forever so it's fortunate that air bubbles trapped by the shifting water table escape from cracks on the sea floor at regular intervals.

Given the dangers that already existed Robotnik didn't have to exercise his imagination too much – sinking the inevitable spikes into the walls, often where the currents were strongest. He also tampered with the aquatic life by, heavily mechanizing the schools of fish and crustaceans which inhabited the ruins. Anyone taking a swim round there was likely to find themselves on the menu of a metal piranha.

CASINO NIGHT ZONE

Mobius's largest city, Robotropolis, sits at the foot of a range of mountains. On its outer fringe lies a sprawling amusement zone of circuses, funfairs and coin-op centres all filled with the most breathtaking and state-of-the-art attractions available: skytrapeze acts, 4D Spinfighter, Neural Ice Collages, a Warpbrain Centrifuge, Blowback tables etc. Back when Robotnik was Kintobor he contributed some games to the amusement zone – machines he put together for his own entertainment. One of his great passions was inventing new angles on an ancient concept called pinball. He'd spend hours of his time constructing two and three tier tables with amazing features. Sonic, too, liked to spend time down there testing his peerless gaming skills against the vast array of machines available. Naturally this all came to a grinding halt when Robotnik's elevator ceased to stop at the top floor. Then he had time for two things and two things only: extending his control over Mobius and spiking Sonic for good.

As he set about his tasteless transformation of Mobius his attention soon turned to the Casino Night Zone. The mad prof liked a gamble – especially when the odds were stacked in his favour, so he decided to work his (black) magic on the place. Also turning it into a death trap suited Robotnik for two reasons: he knew Sonic liked to go there, and, furthermore, the area stood for the one thing he couldn't stand: *Fun.* The thought of anyone actually enjoying themselves sent him into a frenzy of rage and he was

determined to make sure that no-one in their right mind would want to go there. Naturally he dropped in regularly himself.

The happy picture that developed in Robotnik's twisted head was one in which Sonic became a spiky blue pinball being ricocheted off the bumpers or slid off the shoots he constructed into one of the lethal traps he'd conveniently scattered around. His reconstruction of the Casino Night Zone was the work of a man whose brain was permanently on 'tilt'.

HILL TOP ZONE

One aspect of the varied geography of Mobius is its impressive range of mountains whose peaks often poke through the planet's low cloud base. The understated Hill Top Zone features among some of the planet's most spectacular, a collection of table-top plateaus punctuated by huge gorges through which large rivers flow. They make for an impressive sight, even more so since many of the rocks are honeycombed with tunnels and chambers. If Mobius was the kind of place which attracted tourists, which it isn't for obvious reasons, then this would top most itineraries.

It was just the sort of place that appealed to Sonic's exploratory instincts – vast, uncharted and deserted. It was also pretty dangerous too, unstable and prone to sudden earthquakes capable of filling up huge subterranean chambers with lava.

All Robotnik needed to do in a place like the Hill Top Zone was bait the trap and lure Sonic into the most volatile spots. Securing his friends underground in constant danger served that purpose. All that remained was to tamper with the rope platforms and mine some of the chambers to encourage tremors and the job looked to be done.

MYSTIC CAVE ZONE

No one has ever been able to explain the origins of the ivy-covered Mystic Cave Zone which is lit only by flickering insect inhabitants. What is known for certain is that the area has existed almost unchanged for hundreds of years and looks just as it did then. But how it came to exist in its present state has never been resolved by large numbers of scientists who have spent years analysing samples and studying theories. At one point a reward was offered and a title for a scientifically provable solution as to how it evolved. Inspired by the mystery, Kintobor invested much of his time trying to prove his own theory that the first Mobian civilization began in this region.

He asked Sonic to explore the zone and used the hedgehog's findings to propose that a group of natives had joined together there to form the first race. They were intelligent and had the means to make fire, using it to create the lanterns with which they lit the gloom.

Nobody believed him. However, he was convinced he

was correct. Deep in his subconscious Kintobor harboured a grudge . This was unleashed when his personality inverted.

He returned to the zone preparing it for Sonic. Robotnik took it into consideration that Sonic knew the spot well and assumed that he'd be unprepared for the hazards that he placed for him such as spiked brick walls which materialised out of nowhere. He considered with typically grim irony, that Sonic's disappearance would come to be as big a mystery as the zone.

OCEAN OIL ZONE

Way up in Mobius's northern hemisphere there's an island which was once part of a failed economic experiment. Financed largely by a neighbouring planet , it was intended to drill for oil which existed in vast quantities in the area. Planning permission was granted after some dubious dealings and generous deposits in the favour bank.

Construction work began immediately and within months a huge refinery was taking ugly shape with warehouses, rigs, platforms and giant tanks sprawling across a large area. Bore holes were sunk and oil was already being extracted when Mobian environmentalists aided by the genius of Dr Ivo Kintobor saved the day at the last minute.

Protests had been raised as soon as plans for the industrial development became known. After extensive research through historical records Kintobor was able to prove that the site contravened several Mobian laws concerning the sale of planetary resources to other worlds. After a swift court battle the industrialists admitted defeat and retired leaving a large half-finished industrial area behind. Roads were closed and the area remained untouched and totally disused.

Despite trading in his lab coat for a strait jacket Robotnik's memory was still remarkably intact. The zone leapt to his warped mind when he set about transforming Mobius into a giant death trap for his own ends. He rerouted the walk-

ways of the refinery, created disappearing floors and stairways and stationed giant propellers to blast Sonic into well-positioned hazards. He also sabotaged the network of pipes used to carry the oil so that they pumped crude oil straight out into the open causing a giant slick. It was environmental vandalism on a grand scale and it became Robotnik's distorted masterpiece.

METROPOLIS ZONE

Having converted to a direct opposite of himself Kintobor developed a loathing of open spaces, natural scenery, unspoilt countryside and anyone who tried to protect it or live in it. His idea of an arresting view consists of sights like a six-lane motorway under construction, building sites, slum tenements, scaffolding and a factory belching black fumes into the sky.

Accordingly he felt most at home amongst the smog, and high rises of a city, of Robotroplis, a sprawling urban development that Robotnik chose as his capital. He used the enormous wealth he had accrued and the threat of extreme violence to buy power and influence. Anyone who opposed him disappeared in the night and ended up hard at work on the Death Egg.

Retreating to the most low rent, down-at-heel area he could find he set up his HQ to direct operations against Sonic. Based in a disused warehouse he set about constructing a set of hazards – a major feat of engineering. Using drawings he had made years previously for a mega-powered engine he linked hundreds of pistons, cogs and revolving cylinders in tandem to mash and pulp anything that came into contact with them. Giant nuts and bolts held whole platforms together populated by Badniks in over-whelming numbers.

The idea was that the many hazards would pulverize Sonic if he ever made it that far. Not that Robotnik ever expected him to… but then that was his mistake.

Robotnik never expected to fail twice. It was inconceivable that Sonic could ruin his masterplan, but after their first

encounter a seed of doubt remained somewhere at the back of his mind – which is why he built the flying fortress. Stationed in orbit over Mobius the Sky Fortress represented Robotnik's last route of escape. But it was just a precaution really. He'd never genuinely need to use the transporter to flee because he was a genius. And Sonic would never beat him. Right?

SAYONARA, SONIC

Way to go, Blue Boy.
That's the story so far.
Sonic may have defeated
Robotnik in Sonic II, but
we've a nasty feeling the
pyschotic prof will soon be
back. 'Whatever, Sonic'll
be ready, no matter what
the dotty Doc dreams up.
In the meantime, old Blue
Spikes can just chill out,
munch nachos and fries,
speed around Mobius and
generally be one hip dude
hedgehog.

But what of the future?
Who cares says Sonic.
'When you're as fast as I am
you're practically there
already. And once you've
got there it's time to move
on.'

Sayonara, Sonic.

COMING SOON FROM FANTAIL

SONIC TM
THE HEDGEHOG

ADVENTURE GAMEBOOKS

1. METAL CITY MAYHEM

Mobius is under threat from the deranged Robotnik. The demented inventor is busy on a master plan building mega-robots. Only you and Sonic can stop him.

Using your skill, speed and agility, you can help Sonic save the day. But think fast and move quickly, Sonic doesn't hang about and there's no time to waste. The future of Mobius depends on you!

2. THE ZONE RANGERS

Robotnik is turning all the zones into a living nightmare of pollution and destruction. His Mobius Mega Trash Plan can only be stopped by Sonic, Tails and you!

You have to use all your speed, skill and quick wits to help Sonic save Mobius. But time is of the essence, Mobius is decaying with every second. Are you ready for the challenge?